How To Get Wealth From Nothing!

Researched & Written

By

Chris Pickwell

Introduction

A GAME FOR THE 21ST CENTURY GO-GETTER!

An unbelievably simple method that countless people are using, worldwide, to transform seemingly useless items into untold wealth.

Originaly started as a game that people refer to as 'Bigger Or Better', this method has gone on to create some quite remarkable profit margins.

The most famous case is that of Kyle Macdonald, an unasuming and, in his own words 'just an ordinary guy', who nevertheless, over a period of just 12 months, turned a lowly red paperclip he found on his desk into a house... AN ACTUAL HOUSE!

But we'll speak about Guy, amongst others, later in this book... For now, let's learn exactly what 'Bigger Or Better' actually is.....

The Aim Of The Game

The name of the game is, quite literally, 'Bigger Or Better', which pretty much describes it perfectly. When the game was first created it was quite simply that... a game.

The aim of this game in it's basic form was to create teams, either as a party game, a school or college project, or a team building excersize for a company. Each team is allocated some virtually worthless item and must then go out, door to door, and ask people if they have anything they would be willing to swap for it.

It doesn't matter what you exchange your item for as long as the new item that you receive is of a higher value to the one you hand over.... it's that simple! The teams then re-group when their time runs out and whoever has aquired the most valuable item wins the game. It's not unheard of for people to finish the game with a bicycle, or a dvd player, after starting with a pencil stub.

And now, in our wonderful world of convenience, we have the internet... which means that while the world keeps getting smaller and smaller, 'Bigger Or Better' has got much bigger and much, much better.

We'll talk about this a bit later but first it helps, in my opinion anyway, to understand a little thing called 'exponential growth'....

Exponential Growth.

Whilst not being an accurate description of what we are intending, it is nevertheless useful to simplify the formula in one's mind.

let us start with a little story. One that I heard as a child but that infact goes back centuries.

The Chessboard.

Once upon a time, a master craftsman chess board maker hatched a plan to dupe the king out of a fortune.

He started making the finest chess board that the world had ever seen and, knowing the king was both a chess lover and a very greedy king, he made sure that he found out about the chess board.

Once the piece was finished, he was summoned to the palace and, on presenting his work of art, was asked by the king what he wanted for it.

"Your Highness, I don't want money for this. Or jewels. All I want is a little rice."

"Hmm," thought the king, who was a con man himself. "I've got rice. How much rice do you want?"

"All I want," said the craftsman, "is for you to put a single grain of rice on the first square, two grains on the second, four on the third, eight on the fourth, and so on and so on and so on... for the full 64 squares."

"No problem," said the king, not thinking... and he ordered his granary to pay the man for the chessboard.

Well, that turned out to be more than a huge mistake. The first few squares on the board cost the king one grain, then two, then four ... by the end of the first row, he was up to 128 grains.

In the second row things got out of hand. By the 21st square he owed over a million grains... by the 41st, it was over a trillion grains of rice... more rice than he, his subjects or any king anywhere could afford..... by the 64th square he owed more rice than actually existed on the entire planet!

* * * * *

I have calculated all of these numbers and listed them below, if only to show you the enormity of them.... also, bare in mind that i had to do this with pencil, paper and grey matter as no calculator available even comes close to processing numbers this high.....

Square 1; 2 grains

Square 2; 4 grains

Square 3; 8 grains

Square 4; 16 grains

Square 5; 32 grains

Square 6; 64 grains

Square 7; 128 grains

Square 8; 256 grains

Square 9; 512 grains

Square 10; 1,024 grains

Square 11; 2,048 grains

Square 12; 4,096 grains

Square 13; 8,192 grains

Square 14; 16,384 grains

Square 15; 32,768 grains

Square 16; 65,536 grains

Square 17; 131,072 grains

Square 18; 262,144 grains

Square 19; 524,288 grains

Square 20; 1,048,576 grains

Square 21; 2,097,152 grains

Square 22; 4,194,304 grains

Square 23; 8,388,608 grains

Square 24; 16,777,216 grains

Square 25; 33,554,432 grains

Square 26; 67,108,864 grains

Square 27; 134,217,728 grains

Square 28; 268,535,456 grains

Square 29; 537,070,912 grains

Square 30; 1,074,141,824 grains

Square 31; 2,148,283,648 grains

Square 32; 4,296,567,296 grains

Square 33; 8,593,134,592 grains

Square 34; 17,186,269,184 grains

Square 35; 34,372,538,368 grains

Square 36; 68,745,076,736 grains

Square 37; 137,490,153,472 grains

Square 38; 274,980,306,944 grains

Square 39; 549,960,613,888 grains

Square 40; 1,099,921,227,776 grains

Square 41; 2,199,842,455,552 grains

Square 42; 4,399,684,911,104 grains

Square 43; 8,799,369,822,208 grains

Square 44; 17,598,739,644,416 grains

Square 45; 35,197,479,288,832 grains

Square 46; 70,394,958,577,664 grains

Square 47; 140,789,917,155,328 grains

Square 48; 281,579,834,310,656 grains

Square 49; 563,159,668,621,312 grains

Square 50; 1,126,319,337,242,624 grains

Square 51; 2,252,638,674,485,248 grains

Square 52; 4,505,277,348,970,496 grains

Square 53; 9,010,554,697,940,992 grains

Square 54; 18,021,109,395,881,984 grains

Square 55; 36,042,218,791,763,968 grains

Square 56; 72,084,437,583,527,936 grains

Square 57; 144,168,875,167,055,872 grains

Square 58; 288,337,750,334,111,744 grains

Square 59; 576,675,500,668,223,488 grains

Square 60; 1,153,351,001,336,446,976 grains

Square 61; 2,306,702,002,672,893,952 grains

Square 62; 4,613,404,005,345,787,904 grains

Square 63; 9,226,808,010,691,575,808 grains

Square 64; 18,453,616,021,383,151,616 grains

.....Bloody hell!... I'm out of breath now!

These numbers blast past the millions, kiss goodbye to the billions, and smash their way through the trillions.... they then briefly visit the quadrillions before reaching numbers that i don't even know the names of!

Put in another context, if you took just $1, and doubled your money each day for thirty days, then after just one month you will have made $1,074,141,824..... In other words that's one billion, seventy four million, one hundred and forty one thousand, eight hundred and twenty four dollars..... mental!!

I, myself, experimented with this to a limited extent. I chose, as is always advisable, to trade in something that i would enjoy. I opted for that most precious and sought after of antiquities.... vintage starwars toys.

Dealing In Star Wars Toys

I started by making a £10 winning bid on a small job lot of nine figures on ebay. I then went on to split up this small collection and re-sell them as individual auctions back on ebay. A month later, after deducting expenses, I had approximately doubled my money.

x2 =

Now with £20 to spend I immediately blew the lot on another auction consisting of twenty-one vintage starwars figures, and again split them and re-listed them as individual auctions.... which gave me a month to play with them... such fun!

Five months later I'd made £337.50. This exersize was thouroughly enjoyable, and obviously profitable but, unfortunately, it was also unsustainable. Their are neither enough sellers nor enough potential buyers to keep up this business model on ebay alone. But had I completed one year of this venture I theoretically would have made more than £40,000!... wouldn't that be lovely.

But, as I've discovered, these kinds of numbers can send you a little insane if you spend too much time thinking about them. So think in smaller, manageable amounts. By that i mean that it's okay to think in the simple frame of doubling your money with each exchange, but not every day. Rather you should set yourself a more achievable target such as doubling weekly, fortnightly, or even monthly.

That said, if any of you lovely people out there do discover a system that doubles your money on a daily basis, feel free to drop me a line and share your secret.

Tales Of Success

Red Paperclip - A House:

The most famous success story of 'Bigger Or Better' is that of Kyle Macdonald. Kyle was a resident of Vancouver, Canada, he was down on his luck, and he needed a miracle. He noticed an ordinary red paperclip sitting on his desk and BAM!... an idea formed in his mind... He decided he would use the paperclip to play 'Bigger Or Better' online and turn this worthless piece of stationary into a house.

This is what he posted:

This red paperclip is currently sitting on my desk next to my computer. I want to trade this paperclip with you for something bigger or better, maybe a pen, a spoon, or perhaps a boot.

If you promise to make the trade I will come and visit you, wherever you are, to trade.

Hope to trade with you soon!

Kyle

PS

I'm going to make a continuous chain of 'up trades' until I get a house. Or an Island. Or a house on an island. You get the idea.

After 12 months of internet bartering, involving 14 individual trades, the 26-year-old completed the deal. He moved from Vancouver into a two-storey, three-bedroom, 1920s farmhouse in Kipling, Canada.

This is how his trades developed:

1 - a red paperclip

2 - a fish pen

3 - a door knob

4 - a coleman stove

5 - a red generator

6 - an 'instant party kit'

7 - a Bombardier Mach 1 snowmobile

8 - a holiday to Yahk

9 - a cube van

10 - a recording contract

11 - a year's free rental in Phoenix, Arizona

12 - an afternoon with Alice Cooper

13 - a Kiss snow globe

14 - a part in the movie 'Donna on Demand'.

15 - a bloody three bedroom house!

Mr MacDonald said:

"I'm really pleased. I've never been to Kipling, but I've seen pictures of the house, and it looks great. It looks perfect."

"I didn't know how I was going to get to my goal of a house, or how long it would take me, or where the house would be, but I figured that if I kept at it, I would get there in the end."

The town of Kipling decided to make the offer for the publicity, Mayor Pat Jackson said: "We are a small community, just over 1,100 people. We are trying to promote tourism. And who knows, maybe someone out there will think this sounds like an interesting town, and decide to move here. That would be just wonderful."

When the town first made its offer, Mr MacDonald responded and entered into negotiations. In the end he won not just a house but the key to the town, and the opportunity to be mayor for one day.

Cell phone - Porsche Boxter

Steven Ortiz, in his late teens, used Craigslist to trade his way up from an old cell phone to a Porsche Boxter! It took him two years of bartering like a mad man, but it appears that the effort was worth it.

His journey from old cell phone to sports car included working his way up to an iPod, then a MacBook Pro laptop. Eventually, Ortiz traded up from electronics to dirt bikes, then cars and trucks, and an SUV.

"A lot of my friends are jealous," Ortiz said. "A lot of my friends come up to me and tell me, 'You want to trade my phone for a car? Try to get me a Ferrari.' I tell them it's not that easy. It takes time and patience, definitely."

Networking

Social networking is an incredibly effective way of attracting potential business of any kind, but nowhere is it more helpful than in the world of 'Bigger Or Better'.

Your sole goal here is to get maximum exposure for your project, and in this modern world of technology it's simply mind blowing how far, and how huge, you can take things from the comfort and safety of your own home.

Listed below are some of the best social networking sites on the world wide web... read their user guides, really learn how they work, and make sure you use them.....

1) Facebook: **900,000,000** - Estimated Unique Monthly Visitors

2) Twitter: **310,000,000** - Estimated Unique Monthly Visitors

3) LinkedIn: **255,000,000** - Estimated Unique Monthly Visitors

4) Pinterest: **250,000,000** - Estimated Unique Monthly Visitors

5) GooglePlus+: **120,000,000** - Estimated Unique Monthly Visitors

6) Tumblr: **110,000,000** - Estimated Unique Monthly Visitors

7) Instagram: **100,000,000** - Estimated Unique Monthly Visitors

8) VK: **80,000,000** - Estimated Unique Monthly Visitors

9) Flickr: **65,000,000** - Estimated Unique Monthly Visitors

10) Vine: **42,000,000** - Estimated Unique Monthly Visitors

11) Meetup: **40,000,000** - Estimated Unique Monthly Visitors

12) Tagged: **38,000,000** - Estimated Unique Monthly Visitors

13) Ask.fm: **37,000,000** - Estimated Unique Monthly Visitors

14) MeetMe: **15,500,000** - Estimated Unique Monthly Visitors

15) ClassMates: **15,000,000** - Estimated Unique Monthly Visitors

.....Remember, it's all about exposure.

Blogging

You are entering the bloggo-sphere!!...

Sorry... too dramatic?... how embarrassing...anyway.....

Blogging, Whilst being another form of networking, gives you the opportunity to develope an online existance with a permanent home. By that I mean that as useful as social networking sites are, and believe me they are indispensible in your mission here, a blog of your own will lend you legitimacy as an online 'trader'.

A blog is a far more stable enviroment for your online posts. They will stay in one place, at one address, so people will always know where to find you, and where to find your items on offer.

Sites like facebook are excellent places to post, but the timelines mean that your posts become less 'accidentally' visable each day, causing you to have to keep re-posting on a daily basis.

But when you do re-post it's worth attaching a link to your blogs on each one.

Below is a list of sites that will help you create your own blogs.....

1) Wordpress
2) Blogger
3) Tumblr
4) Medium
5) Svbtle
6) Quora
7) Postach.ao
8) Google+
9) Facebook Notes
10) SETT
11) Ghost
12) Squarespace
13) Typepad
14) Posthaven
15) LinkedIn Influencers
16) The Fallen Heroes

Negotiation

Believe it or not negotiation isn't a terribly vital skill in the game of 'Bigger Or Better'... People will make you offers for an exchange, you can either take or leave their offer. Don't be desperate and accept a deal that you're unsure about, the only important rule to this game is to end up with an item of increased value on every transaction.

The only exception to this rule is if there's a trade that you want to make, but the other person doesn't want what you've got. You need to find out what they do want to exchange their item for, find someone who's got it, and try and trade with them... even if your item is worth more then it's worth doing it because when you go back to the original trade you'll still be trading up from your original item.

For Example.....

Kyle Macdonald's first trade was for a fish shaped pen... obviously more valuable than a paperclip... he then swapped that pen for a novelty door knob... again a good deal for Kyle... he kept increasing in value right up to his twelfth transaction, when he ended up, incredibly, with 'An Afternoon With Alice Cooper (how cool is that!)... but now he had his eye on something even more unusual, the lead part in the movie 'Donna On Demmand!'... but the director wasn't interested in 'An Afternoon With Alice Cooper', so Kyle did his homework, and it turns out the guy is a collector of snow globes, like a mental collector, thousands of the things. So, and i know this seems crazy, but he finds someone who has a very rare KISS snow globe (KISS the band that is) and he makes the next transaction... he now has the lead role in a movie and, unbeknownst to him, he is but one transaction away from his dream... in just one short year.

So, if it takes a month to make one exchange, then so be it... on the other hand, I've heard of people that have done terrific deads within twenty minutes of posting their item.... The unpredictability of it all is one of the most enticing things about it.

End Game

Hmmm... the end game... how and when to know at exactly what point you should cash out...

To be honest there's no wrong answer. Of course it's good to hold your nerve, push on a little further to make a little more, but the truth is that the time to get out of this game is whenever it feels right to do so.

The team game/school project/team building version of 'Bigger Or Better' is much easier, as you've already decided before you start exactly what time to finish and compare results. But the 'Long Game', the one that made it possible to turn a red paperclip into a three bedroom house, is better if you do as Kyle Macdonald did and decide at the beginning what item it is you want to end up owning.... he wanted a home... and he got one.

DECIDE WHAT IT IS YOU WANT AND GO GET IT!

www.ingramcontent.com/pod-product-compliance
Lightning Source LLC
Chambersburg PA
CBHW040056250526
45473CB00043B/1772